POSTWAR AMERICA
THE CIVIL RIGHTS MOVEMENT

by Connor Stratton

WWW.FOCUSREADERS.COM

Copyright © 2024 by Focus Readers®, Mendota Heights, MN 55120. All rights reserved. No part of this book may be reproduced or utilized in any form or by any means without written permission from the publisher.

Focus Readers is distributed by North Star Editions:
sales@northstareditions.com | 888-417-0195

Produced for Focus Readers by Red Line Editorial.

Content Consultant: Nishani Frazier, PhD, Professor of History and Director of Public History, North Carolina State University

Photographs ©: Gene Herrick/AP Images, cover, 1; iStockphoto, 4–5; Shutterstock Images, 6; MPI/Archive Photos/Getty Images, 8; Bettmann/Getty Images, 10–11, 18–19; Tony Vaccaro/Archive Photos/Getty Images, 13; Don Cravens/The Chronicle Collection/Getty Images, 14; AP Images, 17, 21; ESK/AP Images, 23; Charles Gorry/AP Images, 24–25; Red Line Editorial, 27; Evan Frost/Minnesota Public Radio/AP Images, 29

Library of Congress Cataloging-in-Publication Data
Names: Stratton, Connor, author.
Title: The civil rights movement / by Connor Stratton.
Description: Mendota Heights, MN : Focus Readers, [2024] | Series: Postwar America | Includes bibliographical references and index. | Audience: Grades 4-6
Identifiers: LCCN 2023029095 (print) | LCCN 2023029096 (ebook) | ISBN 9798889980391 (hardcover) | ISBN 9798889980827 (paperback) | ISBN 9798889981633 (pdf) | ISBN 9798889981251 (ebook)
Subjects: LCSH: Civil rights movements--United States--History--20th century--Juvenile literature. | African Americans--Civil rights--History--20th century--Juvenile literature. | African Americans--Social conditions--20th century--Juvenile literature. | United States--Race relations--History--20th century--Juvenile literature.
Classification: LCC E185.61 .S91435 2024 (print) | LCC E185.61 (ebook) | DDC 323.0973--dc23/eng/20230705
LC record available at https://lccn.loc.gov/2023029095
LC ebook record available at https://lccn.loc.gov/2023029096

Printed in the United States of America
Mankato, MN
012024

ABOUT THE AUTHOR
Connor Stratton writes and edits nonfiction children's books. He lives in Minnesota.

TABLE OF CONTENTS

CHAPTER 1
From Slavery to Jim Crow 5

CHAPTER 2
The Movement Begins 11

VOICES FROM THE PAST
Ruby Bridges 16

CHAPTER 3
Victories and Endings 19

CHAPTER 4
Legacies 25

Focus on the Civil Rights Movement • 30
Glossary • 31
To Learn More • 32
Index • 32

CHAPTER 1
FROM SLAVERY TO JIM CROW

The **civil rights** movement began in the 1950s. But it dealt with old problems. In the late 1400s, Europeans began **colonizing** the world. Soon, they started enslaving people from Africa.

Many enslaved Africans were forced to work in the American colonies. In 1776, these colonies formed the United States.

Colonization and slavery created huge wealth for Europeans but led to the brutal treatment of human beings.

 Before the Civil War, approximately four million Black Americans lived in slavery.

However, slavery continued across much of the country. It ended after the US Civil War (1861–1865).

At first, the US government supported newly freed Black Americans. This period was called Reconstruction. But many white people opposed Black freedom. They used violence. US soldiers went to the South and limited this violence. As a result, many Black Americans began voting. Some became lawmakers.

By the 1870s, fewer leaders supported Reconstruction. US soldiers left the South in 1877. Reconstruction ended quickly. White leaders created a system called Jim Crow. This system borrowed from Northern laws. It denied Black Americans their civil and economic rights. Some laws forced **segregation** based on race. Other laws stopped Black people from voting. Racist violence helped maintain this system.

Many Black Americans protested these unfair practices. They created groups

 Marches were one of the many methods Black Americans used to call for change.

such as the National Association for the Advancement of Colored People (NAACP). This group was formed in 1909. It worked to stop violence and **discrimination** against Black people.

Even so, millions of Black people left the South in the 1900s. They moved to

Northern cities. They hoped for safer, freer lives. This movement was called the Great Migration. Black Americans gained political power. Yet they still faced racism. By the 1940s, Black people were organizing across the country. The civil rights movement was about to begin.

AFTER THE WAR

More than one million Black Americans served in World War II (1939–1945). However, they often faced racism. After the war, the US government helped returning soldiers. But Black Americans were often left out. During this same period, many African countries won independence. Black Americans were inspired. These experiences shaped a new era of Black activism.

CHAPTER 2
THE MOVEMENT BEGINS

Civil rights groups wanted to end discrimination and protect people's rights. They took a variety of actions. One way used the courts. For example, many schools refused to accept Black students. The NAACP worked to change this. In the late 1940s, Black parents tried to send their children to certain schools.

Thurgood Marshall (center) was a lawyer who worked for civil rights. He later became the first Black member of the US Supreme Court.

The schools refused. So, the NAACP sued. The case was called *Brown v. Board of Education.*

The case went to the US Supreme Court. In 1954, the court sided with the NAACP. The court said school segregation went against the US **Constitution**.

Despite this victory, racist violence continued. In August 1955, two white men in Mississippi murdered Emmett Till. Emmett was a 14-year-old Black child. The men who murdered him went on trial. An all-white jury found them not guilty.

Protests continued, too. One began in 1955 in Montgomery, Alabama. The

White bus drivers sometimes drove away without Black riders who had paid their fares.

city's buses were segregated. Black riders had separate seating. They also faced violence and disrespect. In response, a woman named Rosa Parks refused to sit in separate seating.

Many people supported Parks. They began the Montgomery bus boycott.

 During the Montgomery bus boycott, many people simply walked.

A boycott is a type of protest. People stop buying a good or service. In this case, Black people stopped using the city's buses. They wanted Montgomery to change its laws. A new leader also emerged during this time. Martin Luther King Jr. spoke in support of the boycott.

In June 1956, the Supreme Court made another important ruling. It said segregation on buses went against the Constitution. The boycott ended later that year. Black people rode **integrated** buses in Montgomery for the first time.

The next year, *Brown v. Board* was tested in Little Rock, Arkansas. Nine Black students were supposed to attend an all-white school. But many white residents wanted to stop them. Angry crowds gathered at the school. The state's governor also tried to keep the students out. Eventually, the US president sent soldiers. The soldiers led the Black students into school.

VOICES FROM THE PAST

RUBY BRIDGES

Ruby Bridges was born the same year as the decision on *Brown v. Board of Education*. Ruby turned six in 1960. However, schools in New Orleans, Louisiana, were still segregated. Ruby changed that. In November 1960, she became the first Black student to integrate a US elementary school. US marshals took her to and from school every day to keep her safe.

Thousands of people showed up on her first day. "I saw barricades and police officers and just people everywhere," Bridges said. But she thought they were part of a parade. "I had no idea that they were here to keep me out of the school."[1]

Some protesters shouted racist names at her. "They didn't see a child," Bridges said. "They saw change, and what they thought was being taken from them."[2]

US marshals walk with Ruby Bridges as she leaves school in November 1960.

Even so, Ruby continued going to school. The next year, several more Black students started attending the school, too.

1. Phil Bertelsen, director. *The African Americans: Many Rivers to Cross*. Episode 5, "Rise!" *PBS*. WNET, 2013. Web. 21 Apr. 2023.
2. Ibid.

CHAPTER 3

VICTORIES AND ENDINGS

Widespread protesting took place in 1960. **Sit-ins** happened across the South. They helped end segregation in many stores. The Freedom Rides began in 1961. These rides ended segregation on long-distance buses. Some of the protesters faced racist violence. People saw this violence on the news. More

In May 1961, a racist mob set fire to an integrated bus in Alabama. Local police did not stop the attack.

and more people called for change. The US government felt pressure to act.

This period reached a peak in 1963. Groups planned a big event. It was called the March on Washington. Approximately 250,000 people gathered in the nation's capital. They demanded change.

President John F. Kennedy supported some civil rights demands. However, he was murdered in November 1963. Lyndon B. Johnson became the new president. He helped pass major civil rights laws.

For example, he signed the Civil Rights Act in 1964. This law banned racist discrimination. The next year, Johnson signed the Voting Rights Act. This law

The March on Washington helped lead to the Civil Rights Act of 1964.

aimed to make sure Black Americans could actually vote. It outlawed practices that states had been using to stop Black voters.

Leaders believed more progress was needed. Yet they did not always agree on what was most important. Some groups demanded more than just civil rights. They focused on helping low-income Black communities. Others began opposing the Vietnam War (1954–1975). Leaders also disagreed on methods. Some groups believed in nonviolence. Others believed in armed self-defense.

MALCOLM X AND THE BLACK PANTHERS

Malcolm X was a civil rights leader. He believed Black communities should live separately. He wanted them to help themselves. Malcolm X was murdered in 1965. But his ideas influenced groups such as the Black Panther Party. This group started in 1966. It provided aid to Black communities. It also believed in self-defense.

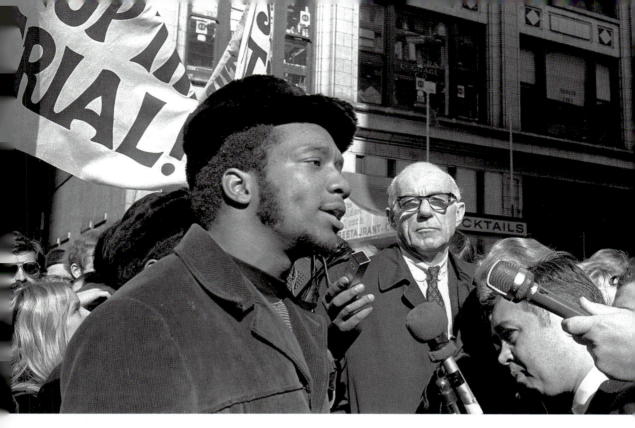

Fred Hampton led the Chicago chapter of the Black Panther Party. In 1969, police killed him while he slept.

Martin Luther King Jr. also focused on many of these issues. In 1968, he went to Memphis, Tennessee. He was supporting Black workers there. But on April 4, 1968, King was murdered. His death was devastating to the civil rights movement.

23

CHAPTER 4

LEGACIES

The civil rights movement had a wide variety of effects. It led to **affirmative action**. Black people began voting in high numbers as well. As a result, the number of Black lawmakers increased. Congress also expanded the Voting Rights Act in 1975. The updated law helped immigrant groups vote.

In 1969, Shirley Chisholm became the first Black woman to serve in the US Congress.

Even so, discrimination remained. It often happened in less obvious ways. For example, news reports talked about Black Americans more often as criminals. Also, police targeted Black people more often. As a result, the number of Black people in prisons increased rapidly.

FAR AND WIDE

The civil rights movement had a massive influence. It inspired movements for Latino rights and Indigenous rights. It inspired movements for gay rights and women's rights. The movement also influenced civil rights groups around the world. It affected other world issues, too. For instance, US groups worked to end South Africa's system of segregation.

In addition, some civil rights gains started going backward. In the 1990s, schools became more segregated again.

BLACK STUDENTS IN MAJORITY-WHITE SCHOOLS

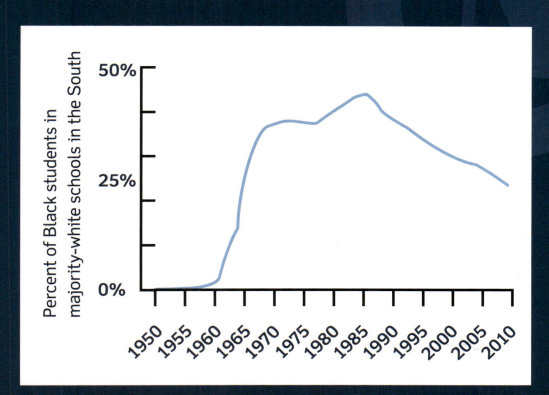

This segregation was not required by law, as it had been under Jim Crow. But its effect was similar.

Barack Obama was elected president in 2008. He became the country's first Black president. For more than 200 years, all US presidents had been white. Many people saw Obama's win as a major outcome of the civil rights movement.

The 2010s showed that the struggle was ongoing. By then, the judicial branch had changed since the 1960s. The Supreme Court started weakening the Voting Rights Act. For example, it ended a part of the act in 2013. This part had kept states from adding racist restrictions.

Black Lives Matter supporters led a worldwide protest after Minneapolis police killed a Black man in 2020.

When it ended, some states passed new limits on voting.

New movements rose up during this time, too. The Black Lives Matter movement spread. It protested police killings of Black Americans. Many of its leaders were inspired by the civil rights movement.

29

FOCUS ON
THE CIVIL RIGHTS MOVEMENT

Write your answers on a separate piece of paper.

1. Write a paragraph explaining the main ideas of Chapter 2.

2. If you could talk to anyone from the civil rights movement, who would it be? What would you want to talk about?

3. When did the US Supreme Court rule on *Brown v. Board of Education*?
   - **A.** 1954
   - **B.** 1960
   - **C.** 1965

4. How can boycotts lead to change?
   - **A.** Businesses may ask the public not to buy their goods or services.
   - **B.** Businesses may enjoy the positive attention that boycotts bring.
   - **C.** Businesses may agree to changes so they'll stop losing money.

Answer key on page 32.

GLOSSARY

affirmative action
Rules that help people who face discrimination. These rules can apply to jobs, education, and other areas.

civil rights
Rights that protect people's freedom and equality.

colonizing
Settling in a new place and taking control, often through violence.

Constitution
The document that lays out the basic beliefs and laws of the United States.

discrimination
Unfair treatment of others based on who they are or how they look.

integrated
Including people of different races.

segregation
The separation of groups of people based on race or other factors.

sit-ins
Protests in which people refuse to leave a place until specific changes happen.

TO LEARN MORE

BOOKS

Harris, Duchess, with Heather C. Hudak. *Rosa Parks Stays Seated*. Minneapolis: Abdo Publishing, 2019.

Kaiser, Emma. *Protests*. Mendota Heights, MN: Focus Readers, 2022.

Lewis, Cicely. *Focus on Civil Rights Sit-Ins*. Minneapolis: Lerner Publications, 2023.

NOTE TO EDUCATORS

Visit **www.focusreaders.com** to find lesson plans, activities, links, and other resources related to this title.

INDEX

Black Lives Matter, 29
Black Panther Party, 22
Bridges, Ruby, 16–17
Brown v. Board of Education, 12, 15, 16

Civil Rights Act, 20
Civil War, 6

Jim Crow, 7, 28

King, Martin Luther, Jr., 14, 23

March on Washington, 20
Montgomery bus boycott, 13–15

National Association for the Advancement of Colored People (NAACP), 8, 11–12

Obama, Barack, 28

Parks, Rosa, 13

Reconstruction, 6–7

segregation, 7, 12–13, 15, 16, 19, 26–28
sit-ins, 19
Supreme Court, 12, 15, 28

Till, Emmett, 12

Voting Rights Act, 20, 25, 28

World War II, 9

Answer Key: 1. Answers will vary; 2. Answers will vary; 3. A; 4. C